SCOOBY-DOO!™

HOW TO DRAW

THIS BOOK IS PACKED WITH LOTS OF
IMAGES TO DRAW. GRAB YOUR PENCIL AND GET
READY TO LEARN TO DRAW SCOOBY AND THE GANG!
YOU COULD GET TOGETHER WITH YOUR FRIENDS AND
MAKE UP YOUR OWN SCOOBY CARTOONS!

GETTING STARTED

DRAWINGS ARE BASICALLY JUST A BUNCH OF DIFFERENT LINES AND SHAPES ALL STRUNG TOGETHER. CAN YOU SNIFF OUT A REASON FOR SKETCHING LINES AND SHAPES LIKE THESE?

THEY'RE THE BEST WAY TO WARM UP FOR DRAWING SCOOBY AND THE GANG.

THE FIRST CLUE

READY TO BEGIN? LET'S START BY DRAWING SCOOBY'S HEAD. ITS EASY! JUST FOLLOW THE SIMPLE CLUES (OR STEPS IN THIS CASE) TO SOLVE THE MYSTERY OF HOW TO DRAW SCOOBY AND THE GANG!

LIGHTLY SKETCH THE BASIC SHAPES IN THE MIDDLE OF YOUR PAPER (SO YOU DON'T RUN OUT OF ROOM).

EACH NEW STEP APPEARS IN PURPLE, SO DRAW THE PURPLE LINES YOU SEE.

REFINE THE LINES ON YOUR DRAWING AND ADD THE DETAILS.

JUST BE SURE TO
KEEP YOUR ARM LOOSE AND RELAXED,
AND DRAW WITH YOUR WHOLE ARM,
NOT JUST YOUR WRIST.

4

5

DARKEN THE LINES YOU
WANT TO KEEP AND ERASE
THE REST.

COLOUR IN YOUR
GROOVY DRAWING!

THE GANG'S ALL HERE

USUALLY THE TEENAGE MEMBERS OF MYSTERY, INC. ARE THE ONES PUTTING THE CROOKS IN A LINE UP - BUT THIS LINE UP IS ACTUALLY A HANDY TOOL. WHEN CARTOONISTS DRAW, THEY PAY CLOSE ATTENTION TO A CHARACTER'S PROPORTIONS (THE SIZES OF THINGS COMPARED WITH OTHER THINGS AROUND THEM). TO CHECK THE PROPORTIONS, ARTISTS USE THE CHARACTER'S HEAD AS A UNIT OF MEASUREMENT. EACH LINED SECTION OF THIS CHART IS ONE HEAD HIGH.

SCOOBY-DOO
THIS LOVABLE GREAT DANE IS QUICK TO COWER IN SCARY SITUATIONS, BUT HE ALWAYS COMES THROUGH IN THE END. WHEN HE'S ON ALL FOURS, HE'S AS TALL AS VELMA IS.

SHAGGY
SCOOBY'S BEST FRIEND AND HUNGRY SIDEKICK, SHAGGY, HAS LONG ARMS REACHING ALMOST TO HIS KNEES. AND HE'S ABOUT ONE HEAD TALLER THAN SCOOBY.

DAPHNE
PRETTY, SMART AND CURIOUS, DAPHNE CAN HOLD HER OWN WITH THE GUYS - AND SHE'S ALMOST AS TALL AS THEY ARE. HER LONG LEGS MAKE HER TALLER THAN VELMA.

VELMA
VELMA MAY BE PETITE, BUT SHE'S NOT SHORT ON LOGIC. IT'S HER BRAINY INSIGHTS THAT USUALLY SOLVE THE MYSTERY. HER HEAD JUST ABOUT REACHES FRED'S SHOULDERS.

FRED
CATCHING CROOKS AND CHASING VILLAINS COMES EASILY TO THIS HANDSOME GUY. FRED IS PRACTICALLY FEARLESS - AND ONE OF THE TALLEST OF THE BUNCH!

SCOOBY-DOO

SCOOBY-DOO IS ONE AMAZING POOCH - HE CHASES BAD GUYS, UNCOVERS EVIL PLOTS AND GOBBLES UP MOUNTAINS OF JUNK FOOD, ALL IN A DAY'S WORK! EVEN THOUGH HAUNTED CASTLES AND SPOOKY SUNKEN SHIPS FREAK SCOOBY OUT, VELMA CAN USUALLY CONVINCE HIM TO GET TO WORK BY OFFERING HIM A SCOOBY SNACK.

ONE EYE IS SLIGHTLY LONGER THAN THE OTHER.

START WITH EGG SHAPES...

...LET THE IRISES BREAK THE OUTLINES.

1

LIGHTLY BLOCK IN THE BASIC SHAPES OF SCOOBY'S HEAD AND BODY. THEN CONNECT THE SHAPES WITH CURVED LINES.

2

NOW ADD HIS TAIL, EARS, COLLAR AND I.D. TAG. LIGHTLY DRAW HIS FACE AND START REFINING YOUR LINES.

SCOOBY'S PAWS CAN LOOK LIKE A HUMAN'S HANDS...

...OR LIKE A DOG'S PAW.

THE UNDERSIDE ALWAYS SHOWS THE PAD.

HIS EARS ARE SORT OF SHAPED
LIKE FORTUNE COOKIES.

THEY'RE NORMALLY
FLOPPY AND BENT...

...UNLESS HE'S
SCARED OR
SURPRISED!

3

SKETCH IN SCOOBY'S
EYES, EYEBROWS
AND WHISKERS.
NEXT ADD HIS
SPOTS, HIS FOOTPAD
AND HIS INITIALS
ON HIS TAG.

4

FILL IN HIS SPOTS
AND HIS NOSE.
THEN ERASE ANY
PENCIL LINES YOU
DON'T NEED.

5

NOW YOU'RE READY TO COLOUR HIM IN! DON'T
FORGET THE CURVED ACTION LINES THAT SHOW
THAT HE'S WAVING!

SHAGGY

THIS SCRUFFY GUY IS MORE OF A
SCAREDY-CAT THAN SCOOBY-DOO IS!
SHAGGY IS ALWAYS A LITTLE
RELUCTANT TO TAKE RISKS WITH THE
REST OF THE TEAM, BUT EVENTUALLY
HE PITCHES IN AND HELPS TO SOLVE
THE MYSTERY.

FROM THE BACK, SHAGGY'S NECK
GETS WIDER AT THE BOTTOM.

1

LIGHTLY DRAW A
GUIDELINE TO PLACE SHAGGY'S UPPER
BODY. ADD AN OVAL FOR HIS HEAD
AND GUIDELINES FOR HIS FEATURES.
DRAW CIRCLES FOR HIS SHOULDERS,
ELBOWS AND KNEES. THEN LIGHTLY
SKETCH THE BASIC SHAPES OF HIS
SHIRT, PANTS AND SHOES.

2

ADD HIS MOP OF
SHAGGY HAIR. NEXT SKETCH
THE OUTLINES OF HIS FEATURES
AND ADD BAGGY SLEEVES ON HIS
ARMS. THEN START LIGHTLY
REFINING ALL YOUR OUTLINES.

3

NOW SKETCH IN
THE LITTLE DETAILS THAT
MAKE SHAGGY COMPLETE,
INCLUDING SEVERAL SHORT
WHISKERS ON HIS CHIN.

SHAGGY'S HEAD JUTS FORWARD WHEN YOU DRAW HIM FROM THE SIDE.

HIS WHISKERS STICK STRAIGHT OUT FROM HIS CHIN.

HIS HAIR IS THICK AND HAS A COWLICK.

DARKEN YOUR OUTLINES AND ERASE ANY PENCIL LINES YOU DON'T NEED.

IS IT LUNCH TIME? SNACK TIME? NO – IT'S TIME TO COLOUR HIM IN!

SHAGGY & SCOOBY

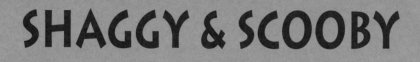

THESE TWO PALS HAVE DONE IT ALL - THEY'VE UNCOVERED SPOOKY SCAMS, CAPTURED HUNDREDS OF SINISTER VILLAINS AND SOLVED COUNTLESS CRIMES. BUT THEIR FAVOURITE THING TO DO TOGETHER IS SIMPLE - EAT! SHAGGY AND SCOOBY LOVE TO SCOFF DOWN EVERYTHING FROM PIZZA TO ICE CREAM (AND EVERY OTHER KIND OF JUNK FOOD IN BETWEEN!).

TWO IS BETTER THAN ONE! AS ALWAYS, START WITH LIGHT GUIDELINES, CIRCLES AND SIMPLE SHAPES.

1

LIGHTLY OUTLINE THE FEATURES ON BOTH FACES AND START REFINING ALL THE LINES.

2

3 ADD ALL THE DETAILS THAT WILL MAKE YOUR DRAWING COME TO LIFE.

WHEN SHAGGY AND SCOOBY GET SCARED, THEIR EYES CROSS, THEIR EYEBROWS ARCH AND THEIR MOUTHS OPEN WIDE.

SCOOBY AND SHAGGY ALWAYS HAVE BAGS UNDER THEIR EYES - FROM WORRYING!

USE STRAIGHT ACTION LINES TO SHOW FRIGHT.

4

ERASE THE LINES YOU DON'T NEED AND DARKEN THE LINES YOU WANT TO KEEP.

5

NOW ALL THAT'S LEFT IS TO COLOUR THESE BEST FRIENDS!

LET'S FACE IT

LEARNING TO DRAW THE EXPRESSIONS OF A CHARACTER ARE AS IMPORTANT AS THE OUTLINES. SCOOBY'S ANIMATED FACE SHOWS WHETHER HE'S FEELING SUAVE, SHY OR SCARED!

1 START WITH THE BASIC SHAPES.

SCOOBY TAKES ON MANY PERSONALITIES.

FROM THINKER...

2 REFINE YOUR LINES AND ADD THE DETAILS

...TO SHOW DOG!

3 ERASE YOUR GUIDELINES AND COLOUR HIM IN!

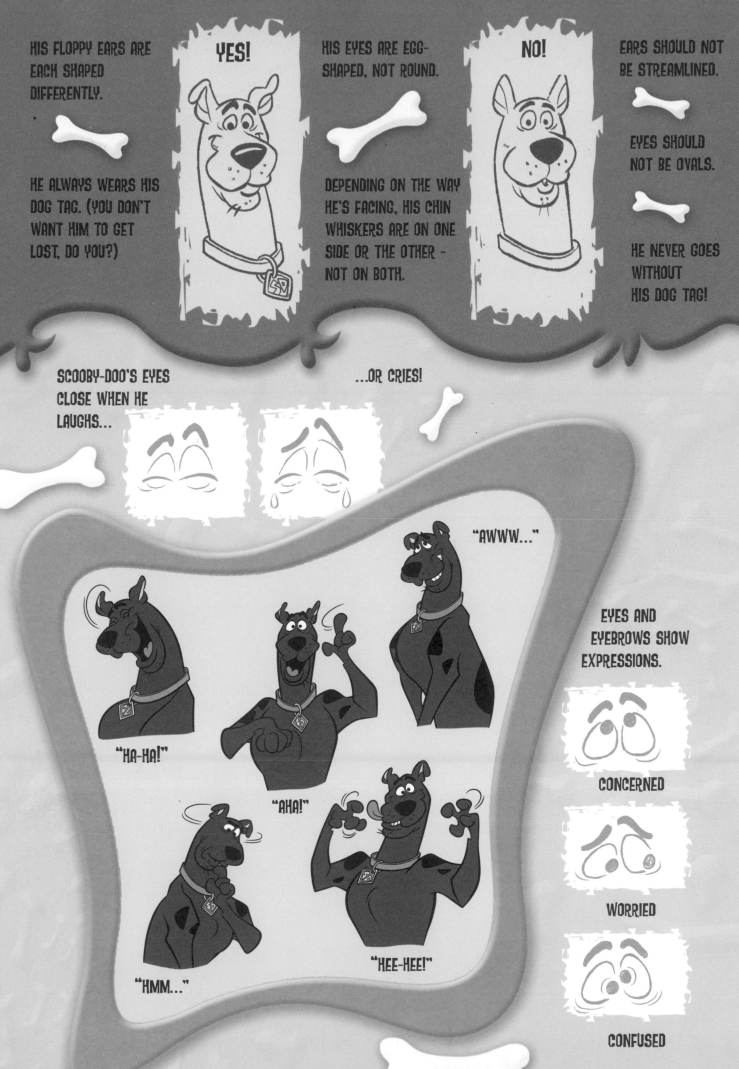

HIS FLOPPY EARS ARE EACH SHAPED DIFFERENTLY.

HE ALWAYS WEARS HIS DOG TAG. (YOU DON'T WANT HIM TO GET LOST, DO YOU?)

YES!

HIS EYES ARE EGG-SHAPED, NOT ROUND.

DEPENDING ON THE WAY HE'S FACING, HIS CHIN WHISKERS ARE ON ONE SIDE OR THE OTHER - NOT ON BOTH.

NO!

EARS SHOULD NOT BE STREAMLINED.

EYES SHOULD NOT BE OVALS.

HE NEVER GOES WITHOUT HIS DOG TAG!

SCOOBY-DOO'S EYES CLOSE WHEN HE LAUGHS...

...OR CRIES!

"AWWW..."

"HA-HA!"

"AHA!"

"HMM..."

"HEE-HEE!"

EYES AND EYEBROWS SHOW EXPRESSIONS.

CONCERNED

WORRIED

CONFUSED

13

DAPHNE

THERE'S NOTHING DAPHNE LOVES MORE THAN A GOOD MYSTERY, BUT HER CURIOUS NATURE OFTEN LEADS HER RIGHT INTO TROUBLE! SHE ALWAYS SEEMS TO BE THE FIRST ONE TO FALL THROUGH A TRAP DOOR OR RUN SMACK INTO A CREEPY CREATURE. GOOD THING HER MYSTERY, INC., FRIENDS ARE ALWAYS THERE TO BAIL HER OUT!

DAPHNE'S LEGS ARE NARROW AT THE KNEES AND ANKLES.

DRAW CURVED LINES FOR KNEECAPS.

SHOES HAVE POINTY "BOWS".

DAPHNE HAS LONG, SLENDER ARMS...

...AND SLIM FINGERS.

1

START DRAWING DAPHNE THE SAME WAY YOU STARTED SHAGGY - WITH LIGHT GUIDELINES, CIRCLES AND OVALS. SKETCH IN THE OUTLINES OF HER ARMS, DRESS, LEGS AND SHOES.

2

USE SIMPLE SHAPES FOR DAPHNE'S HAIR, SCARF AND THE TOPS OF HER SHOES. SKETCH IN A FEW LINES FOR HER FACIAL FEATURES AND REFINE ALL THE OUTLINES.

14

DAPHNE EXPRESSES EMOTION
THROUGH HER EYES AND MOUTH -
AND THE TILT OF HER HEAD.

SURPRISED

SMUG

SOMETIMES SHE
GETS REALLY
SCARED!

SHORT, STRAIGHT ACTION
LINES SHOW FRIGHT.

3

NOW JUST ADD
THE DETAILS TO COMPLETE
HER FACE AND BODY AND ADD PIZZAZZ
TO HER OUTFIT. TWO STRAIGHT LINES
WILL FINISH OFF HER SHOES.

ERASE ALL YOUR GUIDELINES TO
MAKE YOUR DRAWING COMPLETE!

4

5

NOW COLOUR IN THIS
FASHION PRINCESS WITH
PURPLE, PINK AND
NEON GREEN.

15

VELMA

EVEN THOUGH VELMA IS THE YOUNGEST MEMBER OF THE GROUP, THIS CLEVER TOMBOY IS ALSO THE MOST LOGICAL. SHE SEEMS TO HAVE A KNACK FOR PUTTING THE CLUES TOGETHER, AND SHE LOVES TO BE THE FIRST TO EXCLAIM, "I THINK WE'VE GOT OUR MYSTERY SOLVED!"

DRAW TWO CURVED LINES FOR VELMA'S KNEECAP IN PROFILE.

MAKE TWO LINES FOR THE TOPS OF HER SOCKS.

HER THICK CALVES TAPER TO THINNER ANKLES.

SHE HAS A BUTTON ON THE OUTSIDE OF EACH SHOE.

VELMA'S ARMS ARE THICK AND SHORT...

...AND HER FINGERS ARE A LITTLE SHORTER THAN DAPHNE'S.

VELMA STARTS OUT A LOT LIKE DAPHNE - MAKE HER HIPS WIDER AND SKETCH BIG, PUFFY SLEEVES FOR HER POLONECK SWEATER.

DRAW HER HAIR AND A FEW LIGHT LINES FOR HER FEATURES AND SQUARE-SHAPED SPECTACLES. REFINE THE OUTLINES AND ADD THE TOPS OF HER SOCKS.

16

VELMA'S MOUTH AND THE SHAPE OF HER EYES ARE THE KEY TO HER EMOTIONS.

SCARED

SHOCKED

HAPPY

PLEASED

HER SHORT, BOBBED HAIR SWEEPS FORWARD IN PROFILE.

HER POLONECK COLLAR COMES OUT TO HER CHIN.

HER SPECTACLES BECOME NARROW RECTANGLES.

THE BOTTOM OF HER HAIR IS ROUNDED FROM THIS VIEW, AND HER COLLAR IS SLIGHTLY NARROWER THAN HER HAIR.

3

TOP HER OFF WITH A FEW DETAILS, LIKE THE PLEATS IN HER SKIRT AND THE FOLDS IN HER SLEEVE. DON'T FORGET HER FRECKLES!

YOU KNOW THE DRILL - ERASE ANY EXTRA LINES.

4

5

NOW SHE'S READY FOR SOME FABULOUS COLOUR!

FRED

THIS HANDSOME, ALL-AMERICAN GUY LOVES TO THINK UP INVENTIONS THAT WILL HELP THE TEENS SOLVE A MYSTERY. AS THE LEADER OF THE GROUP, FRED OFTEN DESIGNATES RESPONSIBILITY BY SAYING, "LET'S SPLIT UP, GANG!" (ALTHOUGH SOMEHOW HE ALWAYS ENDS UP PAIRING HIMSELF WITH DAPHNE!)

FRED'S THICK, BLOND HAIR "POUFS" OVER HIS FOREHEAD IN PROFILE VIEW.

HE HAS A STRONG JAW AND A THICK, ATHLETIC NECK.

HIS SCARF STICKS OUT PAST HIS CHIN.

SKETCH FRED'S HAIR, COLLAR AND SCARF. ADD THE OUTLINES OF HIS FEATURES AND REFINE ALL YOUR LINES.

2

1

USE STRAIGHT GUIDELINES FOR THIS FRONT-VIEW POSE. FRED HAS WIDE SHOULDERS AND NARROW HIPS. HIS BELL-BOTTOM PANTS REALLY FLARE OUT.

FRED'S MOUTH AND EYEBROWS ARE VERY EXPRESSIVE.

CONFIDENT

FRIGHTENED

HAPPY

SCARED

FROM THE BACK, HIS NEAT HAIR FALLS BELOW HIS EARS.

HIS COLLAR IS WIDER THAN HIS NECK.

HIS SHOULDERS ARE VERY BROAD.

3

WHAT'S NEXT? HERE'S YOUR FIRST CLUE: "AN ERASER WILL DO!"

FRED'S HANDS ARE BLOCKIER THAN THE GIRLS' ARE, MAKING THEM LOOK STRONG AND MASCULINE.

HIS PANTS ARE BELL-BOTTOMS.

4

DRAW THE DETAILS TO COMPLETE FRED'S PREPPY ATTIRE. THEN FINISH HIS FACE AND HIS HANDS.

5

NOW GRAB YOUR COLOURS AND WRAP IT ALL UP!

HIS SHOES HAVE A STRAP ON TOP AND A BUCKLE ON THE OUTSIDE.

THE GANG

NO MATTER WHAT THEY DO, THE MYSTERY, INC., GANG CAN'T AVOID STUMBLING OVER SPOOKY SURPRISES. THEY DON'T SEEM TO MIND THE DRAMA THOUGH, AND THEY HAVEN'T BEEN STUMPED BY A CROOKED PLOT YET!

1

DRAWING THE GANG IS AS EASY AS 1-2-3! START IN THE MIDDLE WITH SCOOBY AND STICK WITH SIMPLE LINES AND SHAPES. REMEMBER TO KEEP THE PROPORTIONS CORRECT!

REFINE YOUR LINES, ADD ALL THE DETAILS,
AND ERASE ANY GUIDELINES.

COLOUR THE CREW AND THEY'RE READY FOR ANOTHER MYSTERIOUS ADVENTURE!

THE MYSTERY MACHINE

COVERED WITH PSYCHEDELIC DAISIES AND FUNKY WAVES, THIS GROOVY CLUEMOBILE IS THE GANG'S FAVOURITE MODE OF TRANSPORTATION. TONS OF COMPUTERISED CONTROLS AND HIGH-TECH SURVEILLANCE EQUIPMENT IS PACKED INSIDE, AND IT HAS EVEN BEEN TRANSFORMED INTO A PLANE.

FOR EACH FLOWER, BEGIN WITH AN X,

ADD A LINE DOWN THE CENTRE.

DRAW A CIRCLE IN THE MIDDLE AND ADD PETALS.

1

THINK "BOX" WHEN YOU START TO DRAW THE MYSTERY MACHINE. BEGIN WITH THREE STRAIGHT, HORIZONTAL LINES AND TWO CIRCLES. THEN DRAW THE SIDE AND SKETCH THE OUTLINES OF THE GANG.

2

LIGHTLY DRAW TWO ANGLED BOXES AND A SWOOSH WHERE THE NAME WILL GO. ADD THE DETAILS ON THE VAN AND REFINE ITS OUTLINES. THEN SMOOTH OUT THE LINES ON THE TEEN DETECTIVES.

3

SKETCH IN THE LETTERING AND ADD THE COOL DECORATIONS. FINISH UP THE DETAILS ON THE SUPER SLEUTHS.

THE DESIGN CONTINUES ON THE FRONT. THE SPARE TYRE IS BETWEEN THE TWO HEADLIGHTS, AND THE FRONT BUMPER IS NARROW.

THE DESIGN ALSO CONTINUES ON THE BACK, AROUND THE TAIL LIGHTS. THE REAR HAS TWO DOOR HANDLES, AND THE NARROW BUMPER HAS A LICENCE PLATE ON TOP.

START WITH TWO SLANTED BOXES AND A CURVED GUIDELINE FOR THE LETTERING.

FILL IN THE WORDS. KEEP YOUR LETTERS LOOSE. IF YOU TIGHTEN UP, THE MISTAKES WILL BE MORE OBVIOUS.

4

LOOK FOR ANY LEFTOVER PENCIL LINES AND ERASE THEM ALL AWAY.

5

COLOUR THE MACHINE WITH BLUE, ORANGE, AND LIME GREEN. LIKE, FAR OUT!

MYSTERY SOLVED!

NOW THAT YOU KNOW HOW TO DRAW SCOOBY AND HIS PALS, YOU CAN KEEP DRAWING THE MYSTERY, INC., GANG IN MANY MORE ADVENTURES. THE SPOOKIER THE BETTER - BUT WHATEVER YOU DO, BE SURE TO HAVE LOTS OF FUN!